# House of Small Absences

for Elliot, Sophia, Phoebe & Luca

# House
# of Small
# Absences

# Anne-Marie Fyfe

**SEREN**

Seren is the book imprint of
Poetry Wales Press Ltd.
57 Nolton Street, Bridgend, Wales, CF31 3AE
www.serenbooks.com
facebook.com/SerenBooks
twitter@SerenBooks

The right of Anne-Marie Fyfe to be identified as
the author of this work has been asserted in accordance
with the Copyright, Designs and Patents Act, 1988.

ISBN: 978-1-78172-240-4
e-book: 978-1-78172-242-8
Kindle: 978-1-78172-241-1

A CIP record for this title is available from the British Library.

The publisher acknowledges the financial assistance of the Welsh Books Council.

Cover painting: A House for Me by Nicola Slattery.

Printed in Bembo by Bell & Bain Ltd, Glasgow.

Author website: http://www.annemariefyfe.com/

# Contents

## I

## II

## III

## IV

# I

*There is no present or future, only the past happening
over and over again – now....*
– Eugene O'Neill, *A Moon for the Misbegotten*

# The Red Aeroplane

From the oratory window I witness
mid-air doom, a slew of concentric
swirls, a trail of forge-sparks,
and that's it. A vermilion two-seater
stagger-wing loops earthbound,
so much depending upon centrifugal
drive. Slivers of toughened glass
spangle the outer stone sill,
the vacant co-pilot seat
is plummeted deep in rosebed mulch.

I question now if the red bi-plane
ever was, the way sureties tilt
and untangle from any one freezeframe
to its sequel. Maybe I was glimpsing
that two-seater red pedal car
– injection-moulded plastic –
collected one Christmas Eve night
for a fevered child? Or conflating
the replica cherry-red sixty-three
we'd toyed with, tinkered with, briefly
on a tinsmith's covered stall
that drenched Saturday?
                                        What can't be
cast in any doubt is the wreckage,
a fragmentary scattering,
the mangledness on the far side
of glass. And how a Galway blue
skyscape proves ineluctably
the exponential function of tangents.

# Kingfisher Days

*The past beats inside me like a second heart....*
       – John Banville, *The Sea*

They amount – spliced end-to-end –
to a flickering of uninterrupted
decades of heady shoreline days,
late-setting evenings and exams finished,
frantic bee stings, the daily island boat,
borrowed bikes to the next harbour town:
with all the drenching, pervasive,
saturate downpours literally obliterated.

# A Trail of Stones

What to make of the latest pattern,
the geometry, the route ahead.

A loudspeaker across the field,
the cattle-trough a disused bath.

The paradoxical maze
of unadopted roads
all lead to the ultimate North,
all run counter to the grain.

# Neuchâtel

Atomisers on their triple-mirrored dressing-tables
dispensed limitless promise: they never failed
to post us oversized birthday cards
with signatures in emerald green ink
and crisply folded bank-notes inside.
                                        They drove
self-starting cars, summered at Neuchâtel,
insisted on keeping lapdogs or Siamese.
How their changing gear with one hand –
mouthing Stuyvesant smoke-rings
out the driver's window – invited admiration!

Not like those aunts in book-club thrillers
who need to slip the serrated steak knives
out of harm's way,
                        who mail cut-and-paste threats
to choristers, Lady Captains and district nurses
newly-appointed.
                        And if you pause a shade before
lighting-up time on a long terraced evening
you just might hear an unscheduled express hurtle
past the town's outer avenues, packed to the luggage-racks
with those same spirited aunts, dashing all the way
down some unmarked siding to god-knows-where,
raising a dry vermouth to their vivid, elegant lives.

# Where Are You Now, Amelia Earhart?

My father would surely have rated
your sheer flight-jacket verve
if you'd ever traded gudgeon pin
gauge sizes in pre-take-off hangar talk.

How you'd have shrugged off his concerns
over the Atlantic attempt, championed
De Havilland *versus* Fokker
in the probable meteorology!

And then he'd have kept a weather-eye
over Parkmore, on harvest-moon nights
just as they'd line beaches in Fiji
or cliff-tops in a Nova Scotia dawn.

How he mused, down the years,
even so, over terse newspaper snippets
about sporadic finds on an atoll,
the zip from a Pittsburgh assembly-line,
your freckle cream jars, travel-size
bottles stamped 'Newark', making sense
of the earlier clues, the flying-fish bones,
the camp-fire ashpits, the rows
of oyster-shells set out to collect dew.

Puzzle for hours until he'd see himself
out there – those exact co-ordinates –
watch as he banks and loops
at under a thousand feet;
as he leans far out of a cockpit
to scan that vast surface for tail-fins,
for a flying-jacket, tiny and distant,
snagged on a stark coral reef.

# The World From Small Windows

Our tool-shed's single window is opaque
with eggshell-finish leftovers, concealing
shovels, dried thistles, a school globe –
seven parts surface water.
                        Out in the stratos
our first cosmonaut charts azimuths,
alignments, his stylus zagging erratically.
A Sopwith's navigator scans Nepalese peaks,
one eye on the shivering gauge.
A tremulous arachnid is latticed
in the angle of a Rio houseboat's casement.

Prospects from such monocular
apertures are ever merciless.

Young widows in our wrung-out seaport
keep vigil by slated, lead-flashing dormers,
seeing that volcanic outcrop rise and rise again
past a fisheye porthole, a blizzarded,
strobing moment, as the horizon
lurches too low for sanctuary.
                        Every one a loser
in the card deck.
                  However you look at it
the county asylum looms ungainly in the finder:
one great, grave, sea-girt hall of sorrows.

At nine-twenty sharp a night orderly stretches
on tiptoe to slide open the observation shutter.

# Honey and Wild Locusts

Tuesday again on Therapy corridor,
the cavalcade starts early: in-patients
shuffle forward in Florentine masks,
eye-patches, beekeeper veils.
                                        Inventory
has a fresh intake of milliners' boxes,
all cranium sizes, a couture range
of spiralled Nile-green turbans.

By evening she's in the wings, her trusted trail
of eggshell fragments leading her back
to the set stage, the spare, clanking bed-frame.

It's a cabinet of overwritten case histories,
lost infancies under key and hasp,
a nether land of biscuit-toned dolls
with identical china-blue eyes.

The maze of concentric circular staircases
rewinds her to the flicker of neon
and another seven days of vaudeville.

Entrée will be stuffed hummingbird
and nasturtiums again. The oversized
circular platters have an odd antiseptic sheen.

# The House at World's End

*Dwelling,* Hiraki Sawa, 2002

Every room in the house congested
with airborne replicas, nose to tail:
Lancasters, Harriers, Messerschmitts.
Late flights are grounded by midnight.
Then radio silence until first light,
when he launches them one by one,
taxiing off from dressing-tables,
worktops, any level surface: watches them skim
mirrors, toothmugs, steers them safely
past lightbulbs, the telltale signs,
small vapour trails across bathroom tiles.
I'm advised to keep my head low,
tune into the sudden close hum,
the waspishness of a tiny Mig fighter.
One by one they learn to adapt
to emergency flightpath restrictions,
the indeterminacy of destinations.

# The Observation Window

*Childhood is the kingdom where nobody dies.*
　　　　　— Edna St. Vincent Millay

I'm not convinced, even now, the planet
revolves under me. I've always known
if I hold my breath the globe will grind to a standstill,
known that if I watch myself
from a capsule's observation window
I'll see a stationary child in Metson's field,
axis and focus of a universal stasis.

# The Outer Provinces of Sleep

The definitive map of insomnia's low on contour-lines.

An initial submerge, then the same neutral shade
from every hour travelled.
                            All over the state
in basement laundries, a million hospital sheets churn.
Night porters gawp at *Deliverance's* closing credits.
                                     Two a.m. –
three – four – the last clutched dog-hours
                                of so many existences.

An out-of-sync clock strikes quarters in an echoey
atrium. The plateau of sleeplessness borders on crimson.

You see yourself slide out Aunt Sarah's cotton-reel tray,
the cards of hooks-and-eyes, the appliqué needles
she'd converse through, tight-lipped, tacking....

Out there: roadkill, poachers, gunlamps. Here: phosphor
clock hands, turbulence, an upturned novel.
                                Now you're back
to an October night, a week-old pup targeted by a blizzard
of irascible wasps while you slept through.
                                It's then you realise
your raftered room's a stage set with one candy-coloured clown
tiptoeing off to solitary applause.
                            In these freighted, anxious
hours, everyone stands in line for indemnity and oblivion.

# Worry Beads

When vigilant planets eclipse us
there's no lucid place to stand. No place
to step up and articulate.
          By omniscient
arclight you measure a day's short-changings,
permeable untruths, indelible lies:
                              in stairway
dark you're chased by howling wraiths
through cycle-racks, over footbridges,
past security barriers. You wrestle the clammy
twisted sheets.
          Bouts of amnesia mutate
in the febrile gaps: unheralded at 3 a.m.,
the glucose ebb, cardiac deceleration,
random seizure, another disconsolate fugue.

Then daylight: and money-off vouchers
litter doorsteps on our wide-awake street.
Select brethren turn indifferent backs
on the rush-hour heading west against the flow,
radios locked on traffic news.

All our cutlery drawers bulging,
cluttered with worry beads.

# Winnower

Everyone can use a listener, who
won't demur, pass judgement, won't
agree necessarily.
                    Everyone, they say,
has their own story to tell.
                    Retelling, you dredge,
filter, embellish. In the final analysis
it was your story all along, it seems.

# II

*When we were ten we found refuge in the attic's timber-work. Dead birds, old bursting trunks, extraordinary garments – the stage-wings of life. And this treasure we said was hidden, this secret treasure of old houses, so wondrously described in fairy-tales – sapphires, opals, diamonds. This treasure which shone softly. The raison d'être of each wall, each beam. Huge beams defending the house against we knew not what. But yes – against time. For time was the arch-enemy.*

– Antoine de Saint-Exupéry, *Southern Mail*

# House of Small Absences

*One need not be a chamber to be haunted…*
*The brain has corridors surpassing*
                    – Emily Dickinson


In her room at the eaves of the world
she's stuck again on the perplexity
of fly papers,
                    mouths what wireless
lyrics are covertly telling her,
                              settles
for sleep, adding the night's thimble
of chalky easefulness to a rattling
Kensitas carton in the going-home bag
she re-packs nightly.
                    A crow flaps
on her window-ledge as the front
gates clank.
                    A last empty cab passes
the keeper's lodge.
                    The hospital grounds'
rusting goalposts haven't witnessed
a single full-time score this past
half-century.
                    A circus of night
and day: *Only you beneath*
*the moon and stars and the sun.*


One returnee picks out only the ebony keys
on an institutionalized Steinway.
                              Every watch
in Saddler's store window-display's gone awry.
Streetlamps flicker before plunging
Town Square in blackness. A distant
twister. Another concentric Dantean circle.


Lights go out window by barred window. Night
and day. Day. Night. *You are the one.*

# Pilgrimage

Like it's a re-run of the Sunday visits,
but once a year, late evening, summer usually.
Perennially unchanged.
                              Tall pines,
'Fifties asbestos roofing on 'The Villa',
the green-varnished veranda chair that's
never used. Silence broken only by rooks.
The tower clock's shown 1.30 for nineteen years.

There's always a lone post-war ambulance
parked up at 'Rosgrove', awaiting the call.

# The Cure

*Confusion is not an ignoble condition*
*— Brian Friel, Translations*

Someone said sleep was the answer.
To a question she'd forgotten. She slept
as graduations, funerals, winters,
came and went; she was sedated,
blurred, anaesthetised. A hinterland
of migraine and neuralgia,
of dank bluebell woods and Saturday
piano lessons with the Sisters.

## Vergissmeinnicht

Unit B's interior has reclaimed
mahogany stair-rails, tentative banisters
against her confusion.
                    The first prescribed
inrush of normality shows no hint
of receding.
                    The facility's gardener
who stamped Ravensbrück permits
on last year's semester break, spends
a day retrieving the year's dead
foliage from the ornamental fountains.

She spends the morning in Occupational
realigning perspectives, the dryness of
porous charcoal setting her skin on edge.

Stark alders are both image and icon
like the orchard of little pine crosses.
Behind the sanitising poplars, beyond
virtuous edifices, past the barbed fence,
lie the incinerators, their peaceable roars
consuming another day's forgetting.

Overwrought charcoal hatchings
on a taut canvas reveal hazy images
of a brief and long-suppressed life....

# Primary Seven

From the cliff-path you can just catch
the clang of the master's bell,
a chorused *Skye Boat Song* on a rising wind:
no duffels on pegs, no stove-smoke,
just high fanlighted windows, ink-stained
pencil grooves on empty desks
where initials were long since
dug deep with a Helix compass-point.

# Headland House

*Once you're an exile your roots have*
*no geography to sink into....*
          – Isabel Allende

There's the same curve in the road
but the arc seems smaller.
As you near, each night, oxygen thins.
There's the same sycamore, the same
red door, unpainted, unlatched.

And your doll's house is still in the attic.

# Salmon Port

I can't recount the footholds,
the rocks are mossed-over and the salmon-hut key's
not under the usual stone
but I can number, through a barred window,
a kettle, two upturned orange crates,
another window that looks back to the town
under its friendly, fierce mountain.

# What the Dead Don't Know

Grows quickly, daily, from the perimeter
of a postage stamp, until it's twice the size
of Norway, and growing fast.

What the deceased can't understand
is why they don't still hear from us
day-by-day, hour-by-hour.

What the departed don't see
is how the lead story has moved on.

What the dead won't say
is more or less what they didn't say
when they had the chance. Diplomacy,
tact, reserve: these things endure.

# Splitting the Atom

A rare November asteroid shower.
Searchlighting the drenched
flagstones of my mother's own streets
under biblical gantries. A future gazer's
twenty-five-twenty-five scope
might yet catch its last pale glint.

Light-years from now. It was how I learned
to read slate-ridges better than death columns,
chiselled marble names, sniper rounds
off the precipitous Limestone Road.

Nightly under goose down I'd pillow-hide
from the phases of moondancing roomlight
that splintered the black. Galvanised
dustbin-lids echoed in overshot alleys.
The blackness of damp, palleted stacks
waiting for the bonfires, the first lit spill.

Blackness that had defeated her.
A corridored room. Manicured grounds.
Plumped-up goose down. The snapping shut
of aster gypsophila clusters in a Melaware jug.
A Ljubljanka of starch-white coats
and stalled ceiling fans.
                         Striking out
on orbits, tangents, rewound neurons,
irretrievably forced landings
on solitary uncharted dark stars.

# Before the Swarm

There's sedative for the entire hive. The hospital
manufactory's on Saturday time churning
glazily marzipanned confections. Smoke's
puffed in at arrhythmic intervals to enhance
perfunctory recall. There's a cloyingness
throughout by chamomile hour.
                              The queen
shivers with recurrent waves of mild remorse
but the novitiate buzz drones on
*ad nauseam.*
                    Stronger intrusions of opiate
are essential to quell the mutinous murmurs.

Outside there's a barrier membrane, thin,
impermeable, milkwhite. Within, gathering
intelligence has the swarm spiralling close.

The cloud-level shoal with their vivid insignia
might yet attempt covert re-entry
through crumbling pre-war mortar before the onset
of evening rounds and the veiled standby
apiarists. The cardiac ambulance hovers
on black-and-yellow zigzags by the automatic doors:
in its sickly wake, a fleet of curtained hearses.

And hardly an arum lily or immortelle in sight.

# Ocean House

A stark flotilla out of a Giacometti
nightscape rounds the basalt outcrop,
clears landfall by a good sea mile.

At Ocean House the incumbents who've long
abandoned sleep, stand gumboot-deep
in rosebed mulch by the shrubbery wall
or lurch out of bath chairs to gaze mesmeric
through the sun-parlour's condensation,
salute the spectre fleet's passing,
wait for the swell's amplitude
to recede to normal.
                    In Tuesday's
post-office they'll deny they ever saw a thing
but they can't lose the clatter of rigging,
the gale-howl of sheets for days. For more days.

The chief coastguard swears he could chart
sidereal time by this apparition. Put it down
to a dreamy miasma if you will
but how to account for the shoals
of dead white flounder scattered round
your sea-washed front-steps at daybreak?

# Clockhouse Terrace

How they long for the pallid sleep
of untroubled minds, to a man!

But some have the melancholy palsy, some
hazarded and lost much: there's one on a first
floor landing who can't decide whether to go up
or descend. The striking clock he smuggled
from Lucerne rebukes him hourly in the glazed hallway.

Betrayals, standard lamps, small infidelities,
wireless valves, christening gowns, are all grist.

The crescent's brisk centenarian plays
Bezique in a yellow-lighted Edwardian parlour,
listens as the shades of coastwise sea-captains
pace the abandoned upper floors again.

The whole row could implode on a spontaneous
sou'westered night, drag all this unfathomed history
down deep. A fortnight's rain is all it would take.

# III

*I had started my own collections. They were kept at home in a cupboard. But inside my skull grew an immense museum and a kind of interplay developed between the imaginary one and the very real one that I visited.*
    — Tomas Tranströmer, *Memories Look at Me*

# No Second Acts

*There are no second acts in American life....*
  – F. Scott Fitzgerald, *The Great Gatsby*

Just when you're sure he's gone
for good, it's Lady Day and he's back,
wind-burnished as Egdon's reddleman,
rootless, tricksterish, his own chancy self's
alter-ego: my faith in him lapsed
lazily way, way back in the azure
yonder and yet he's here again, still,
for tonight, with the bed of nails
and the red satin fez, three along
the nightbus queue for Stillingfleet
and Verdun Road.
                    I see the shiver
that says he knows I know he's still
out there, operating, making
waves, this hearse-bound, some say,
hanger-on, sallow under the Broadway's
streetlamps.
                    He hardly troubles
to conceal the click of secateurs
in his moleskin trousers pocket.

The empty nightbus decelerates
in a sulphurous drumroll spluttering
of exhaust and he's gone, gone for good,
once again, for now.
                    Never in his life owned
to the forwarding address in World's End,
never once stepped on pavement grouting.

## Pièces de Résistance

*Why were we so quickly sated with the happiness*
*of living in the old house?*
       − Gaston Bachelard, *The Poetics of Space*

It's a house that won't ever
open up willingly to new chattels.
Doors could slam unprompted at the precise
moment removers arrive with carbon copies
and pencil stubs, the blood in their arteries
turned glacial by a sudden unwelcome shiver.
It's likely more than one fuse will blow
in the consumer unit before they're through
the vestibule. They'll make a phonecall
or two − despite the problematic signal −
double check there isn't a glitch somewhere,
a misunderstanding over postcodes.

# Nights at the Memory Palace

*To have a childhood means to live a thousand lives before the one.*
*— Rainer Maria Rilke, Letters on Life*

The pop-up cinema appears overnight
on the vacant lot of your childhood.
                                    The enthusiast
behind the projector fast-forwards your narrative
between finger and thumb, unspools reels,
rushes past sand hills, a tartan Thermos, a cliff path,
skytrails, a tipped-over toy-box....
                                    In pre-title
shots we meet your parents, brothers, the missing
Binghamton uncle.
                        Even the soundtrack's
the comforting sadnesses of 'Stranger on the Shore'.

And then that's you in the frame, the hesitant
gestures, you're centre-field, top left, you're
in every crowd scene.
                        There's little resembling
script or plot, but every movie you've seen
is subtly referenced, the screen itself a testament
to recall and divination.
                            A screen that flickers...
stutters to white, then dies. This can't be it. Surely?

Where's the blast-damaged philatelist's shop,
the pre-war Bechstein, the Detroit motel's safety-chain?
What have they done with the curling *Luftpost* stickers,
frayed maps of Antarctica, the Seattle tower-block
incident?
            Where are the manilla postcards,
the *Liégeois* in a small *schloss*?
                                    And oh, what became
of the window-woman in a gas-lit compartment,
bound, in the title sequence, for Voronezh?

# Carpathian Flyer

On the wire-walk of sleeplessness
the neighbour's newest is crying itself blue.

Our Bucharest-bound sleeper jolts
at a remote station-clock's sudden 'TOCK'
then dissolves into white tree-lined delirium.

The physician with sleep apnoea holds his breath
a little shorter after each exhale. He's just
seen his last July slip into a bleak September.

Hollow souls of the seemingly departed
hang over a hundred or so sleeping roofs.

Painted saints in their chipped wooden draperies
pale in the heretic glare of sanctuary lamps,
of draught-flickered beeswax candlelight.

An orphaned snowy owl's lost his night sensors,
finds himself nervily close to the oblivion
of Sunday morning mist and burnt stubble.

A tang of childhood night-times – the shattered
glass, sulphur and gelignite – hangs heavy still.

Our dead revisit in noiseless hours. Invited
or not. And leave us with burnout so intense
we can only risk catnaps for months after.

# The Image of Sainthood

Am I lifesize today? Usually
it's hard to tell, fasting
from midnight. There's a corkscrew
in my cranium, a crucifixion
in both frontal lobes. My halo
is my armour though it might
be mistaken for an old brass salver
from *la maison de ma tante*.
A charm of *brocante*
dangles above either shoulder.
That diminutive cockatiel I acquired
in Caracas fell off his gilded perch
last night. After all those months
of practice he couldn't memorise
a single line of plainchant.
My cardinal-red *galero's* a burden
on this September feast day.

Ah! Now I'm lifesize again
I can risk quitting the *atelier*
for a few lit hours. My beard grows
with the richness of wheatgrass,
the speed of coral. A fresco'd
left foot interrupts my every
contemplation. Yesterday's tracts, tomorrow's
ceiling designs, flutter to the stone flags.
*Look out now the saints are*
*coming through* with our familiar
cluster of sins and epistemologies,
our clutter of egg beaters, hair-springs
and authenticated relics. Let me button
my brocade waistcoat against the grain.

# Hot, Copper Skies

There are watches when you'd pray for a burning deck.

The log-book's copperplate confirms
 you're nine days out and face-to-face with reality.

No trite familiars, just a long unsoundable
Kamchatka of the soul. This sea takes no prisoners.

Nothing tangible, no icebergs, no albatross.
Maybe you were always your own secret sharer.

White's the measure of delirium, the colour
of absent clouds. Dorsal fins circle.

A first mate wishes he'd never learned to swim.
No barter to be had, just the switchback ride
of precipitous seas, arctic portholes, flat calm.

You spend days awaiting captain's orders,
knitting Sargasso weed into porpoise nets,

your crossbow stood in a gunwales corner,
loaded. No omens in telescopic range.

You've even seen the flotilla of jinxed mariners
in tattered smocks, on their doldrums pilgrimage,
seeking a rightful seabed committal.

The moon wrestles with the ocean's desperate
need for stasis, its spite, its ancient obduracy.

Charts are spread. Far corners weighted.
Dividers, compass, calculations. Limitless
options for courses you may never set.

# The Museum of Might-Have-Been

Opens its doors one Sunday a month
in winter. The queues back up for decades.

If you're lucky and your number's called
you can have any tour: *Your Charmed Life,*
*Your Regrets, The Prodigal You,* every second
slip-road at the intersections of the possible.

The exhibits are stark and infinite
under strip neon, long hallways
of lost opportunity, slow clocks,
stopped clocks, rooms where even now
a thought might wither: the attic storeroom
is out-of-bounds to all but the curators,
though artefacts are still donated by the hour.

Standing in line is no guarantee
of admission: some days
word spreads that when you
reach the queue's head, pass through
the double doors, it'll be stripped out,
even lightbulbs, with only packing materials
and discarded drapes left. Yet critics insist
*The Multiple-Choice Foyer, The Roads-Not-Taken*
*Gallery, The Back Burner Café* are stunning.

Every room's a tasteful shade of apple-white
apparently. Waxworks and living statues
rehearse at intervals for *The Balcony Scene,*
*The Shining City, The Reconciliation,* over
and over, night by night. As in the finest operas.

# Red Rooftops

A wordless mutual disquiet
before we'd even parked the rental-car.

Vertigo for miles, claustrophobic peaks.

Then gingham cloths, carafes of iced water,
the sublime manoeuvring in close, early.

At the next table one man has three fingers
missing, a hornhandled hunting knife
in his top pocket. The other hand
has a resting tremor.
                        Surrounded
by women who'd weathered the post-war years
Yevgeny announces, *A thin woman
is a sign of death.*
                        Bullet holes
mark the 16th century citadel's rampart: long-dead
musketmen control the belfry. With the nearest
market town four days off by mule,
facial tics are distressingly alike, the gene pool
dwindling fast in a huddling of traits.

Mudslides, February rockfalls, contagion,
you'd never get a foothold in these rare altitudes.

There's a solemn gaze from shop doorways, café tables,
a people who bury secrets in stone crevasses.
The mountain has them in its louring familial grip:
granite, scree, low cloud.
                        Monique shudders
as the ignition grinds, eyes the rearview
until the third bend on the downward corkscrew
loses the last glimpse of the red jostling rooftops.

# Incremental Weight

*Il faut traîner le boulet de son individualité jusqu'à la fin.*
*(One must drag the ball-&-chain of one's individuality to the very end.)*
            – Joseph Conrad

You argue it's regulation backpack size.
Same black as the others. You're too quick to confirm
you've packed your own. Heartbeat spiking again.

By nightfall, though, it's a fold-out big-top
bursting to be expansive, extravagant –
rows of tiered benching, alpacas, a sell-out.

*Seven was the dawning hour of silver, the glassiest*
*icestorm, ridge impassable with a sealed*
*prison wagon adrift on the turnpike.*

Cab-drivers helped you wrestle it through slush
to the start of the moving walkway while outside
our town's spotlit snow-Kremlin shimmered on meltdown.

The newly-burdened tread water at e-ticket check-ins.
Which superfluous gallery plan, carnet, street finder
will be the final straw, defeat the zipsliders?

*The delusion's that one acclimates to incremental*
*weight. But you hyperventilate on flight-steps.*
*And fight shy of the smug, proffered empathies.*

You've mastered the art of losing these capacious holdalls
in scrubby ravines, perimeter hedges: a patent rigmarole.
There's always a chip with your zip code stitched in the strap.

*In extremis* you've even burgled into unclaimed effects
after hours, hoping someone else's mislaid theirs. Tartan,
maybe. And got away with it. Until the planes strike.

# Rogues' Gallery

When I've been placed on hold
I like to doodle faces, the usual suspects
I've sketched down the years.
Always in profile. Identikits,
mug-shots, line-ups, regular
police-court work. Perhaps
if you could come forward one-by-one
and make yourselves known?

# Post-Industrial

Our small town is nervy with silence
and battery flashlights.
                          The river-silt
offers up a new puzzle daily.


Tom Birt's diesel chainsaw catches
a jagged glint of five o'clock streetlight
as he shoulders it past the general store,
homeward from another day's clearings.


All of us struggle in this low-lying toxic mist.


In our quiet town I pass the evenings
watching for the bonfires, practise
not looking direct into full beams
of passing trucks.
                          Improvised roadblocks
are a nightly occurrence.


                          On Tuesday
I quizzed the Stone Boat's barman
on where to find low-energy C-9s
for my torch, longlifes or rechargeables,
to survive another fall's interminable
depredations. No answer.
                          Down
at Port Douglas the tourist skiffs
are all knee-deep in bilgewater.


Far out by the dead lightship
there's no telling that's not another
stray log from the day's clearings
afloat face-down in the water.

## Camino Real

A bolt from the indifferent gods
flashlighting the high *autostrada:*
in the rearview there's a Lancia
swerving closer than you'd like
but you've no urge now to joust.

Another day, another *auberge*: you're
spooked by the toupée'd sommelier's
remote gaze, the unlidded
bleak fisheye of a freshwater carp,
filmic in capsicum and aspic.

The really shrewd track minutes
on their several watchfaces. But
you find you're starting to exalt
yesterdays over the here and now.
Time to converse with the minor deities.

Check if there's barter to be done.
Your eyelid's been twitching offscale
since the four-thirty alarm-call,
a scenario closely resembling the stage-set
before the *Götterdämmerung* overture.

# Street Scene

*'Nowhere' is a setting, a situation and a state of mind.*
*It's not on any map, but you know it when you're there.*
                            – Don George, *Tales from Nowhere*

When you turn your back on the street
and walk away one block, then two,
the over-familiar street-view's exposed
as propped-up storefronts and verandahs,
sceneries of wings and facades
that could shudder and collapse
in the whish of the tenderest summer breeze.

The scene's drained first of Technicolor
then slips slowly out of focus,
passers-by strutting staccato
into the maze of tram-line junctions
that never make it into a town's gazetteer.

Each new city block takes you further
from the grip of a reality that's already
packing-up shop behind you, shipping
for storage or the next production.
You'd do best to maintain a brisk walking pace.

# Late Rooms

You might also like to check out...

Our rented room in Rue de la Bastille
the summer we turned eighteen: the exoskeletal
cage-lift spooked us for a week.

Gulls – below our Monterey balcony
on tidelined sand – that still remembered Steinbeck,
or at least Doc and his jars of molluscs.

The ten-foot spruce in a recently refurb'd
Wicklow country house, its branches
laden with empty gift-wrapped boxes,
guarded by wolfhounds and an old red setter.

Our gondola-bed in Hotel Do Pozzi
adrift on the darkest canals, a lone lost *traghetto*
rising and falling on its way to the glove market.

The 44th-Street lobby where 'Twenties wits
gathered to parry Parker's thrusts
over last-minute pre-theatre Manhattans.

The Borders 'Scottish Baronial'
with primrose cellular blankets;
the boudoir Amontillado and oranges
set out that last September before rationing.

The Palais Royal hotel where, from our window,
we marvelled at a topiary concert-grand
in the Louis Quinze courtyard, a neatly clipped
Debussy fingering silently sculpted keys. Piped
muzak permeated the Belle Époque restaurant.

And just after the curtain fell in Bratislava
we breakfasted on gelatined eggs while
the concierge frisked delegates for revolvers.

# IV

*...it is like being in an unfamiliar hotel room, where the alarm clock has been left on the previous occupant's setting, and at some ungodly hour you are suddenly pitched from sleep into darkness, panic, and a vicious awareness that this is a rented world.*
    – Julian Barnes, *Nothing to be Frightened Of*

# From the Cockpit Window

*Here, above,*
*cracks in the buildings are filled with battered moonlight.*
          – Elizabeth Bishop, *The Man-Moth*

The full moon is being held hostage
tonight. A two-hundred-&-seventy degree vista
and all I make out are roof-garden umbrellas,
latticed fire escapes, jungles of wisteria
straggling around water-tower struts.

Uplighters cast panther shadows
and Egyptian columns against the cloudswirl
that drapes the Chrysler pinnacle.

There's a low-altitude nosedive, a rattle
of applause on the wing. Our world
is hurtling towards sudden resolution.

Tumbling zeros play needle roulette,
the spirit bubble's way out of kilter.

Close enough now to smell garbage scows,
charred pretzels, onions, to hear
taxis honking, meters ticking,
the steam whoosh of airshafts.

On my tongue there's the aftertaste of metal fatigue.

Who'll answer my entryphone? How long
before they empty the closet of shirts
and jackets, their sleeves hanging aimless.

# Last Order

On the card he ticked the hearty
breakfast, his tribute to all those
dead-man-walking films, though he couldn't
recall any close-ups of the trays
to know if they got eggs-over-easy:
he speculated on God's will, if God
comes into the final scene at all.

Life would go on despite the lack
of a single mourner. No one
who'd know that he'd once felled
forty larch in a day's chain-sawing,
know that his father had wasted
a decent life in a Cleveland abattoir,
his mother gone since the second child?

And the sky wouldn't fall in just because
he'd not returned the Monday library's
only Dostoyevsky, the one he'd not long
started. This morning he'd sensed *rigor*
in his fingertips, folded the corner back
at page twenty-four. And a last wish?

No, not to know in advance if he'd struggle
when they'd strap him to the gurney, how
quick they'd find a prominent vein, know
the proportions of opiate to lethal dose
in the mix. No. Simply to lie awake again
one baking-roof night on top of the old
apartment block, rise at the first traffic noise
to the whirr of Uncle Nathan's coffee grinder.

# Blue Skies, Nothing But Blue Skies

Sidewalk vendors look askance when I ask
*Am I headed East or West?* I could
tell them I navigate by the sky's colour
but it wrong-foots me time and again.
*What sky?* they say, looking up. The one
that cracked wide one bright September,
while we were looking away, the one
that enchanted Portuguese cartographers,
the sky that sheltered a century's huddles,
a parasol over sidewalks, wharves, fire-trucks,
ferry-boats and strings of bulbs on lighted bridges,
over sixteen miles of serene Canaletto clouds.
*No, not any of those...* And yet
all of them. And my pale blue heaven, too,
that I watched from childhood's promontories
on an ocean's edge, miles from the here and now.

# High Wire

*The essential thing is to etch movements in the sky, movements so still they leave no trace. The essential thing is simplicity. That is why the long path to perfection is horizontal.*
          – Philippe Petit, *To Reach the Clouds*

They took away the buildings
when he wasn't looking.
Then the hawser. No need
of a spirit level these days. No winches
for tension. He thrived
on the sharp etiolations of air,
the impossibility of distance.
Didn't ever look down.
Kept on, keeps on, placing
one steady foot in front of the other.

# Our Little Town

*Nothing but the dead and dying back in my little town*
— Paul Simon, *My Little Town*

The whole tidy village of them:
dancing-master, pork-butcher,
dog handler. Bookmarks
in the grass now. Dominoes. Who
in their time stood becalmed
at these same gravel intersections
dwelling on their place in the overall schema
pinned inside the gravedigger's shed door.

# The Window Washers

Forty three thousand six hundred and two
daily challenges: behind the plate glass,
tidy desks, boardrooms, silent water coolers,
anticipate copywriters checking in,
as Manhattan's window washers gather
gloves and overalls, regular gear
on a late summer Fort Greene Tuesday.

A window washer's dream of a sky
but here's one that still slithers the locket-chain
with his mother's relic of St. Stanislaus Kostka
before stepping in the elevator, not that luck's
needed much, now it's a breeze of a job:
cages, platforms, robotics, even,
on the uncomplicated drops; no
more harness anchors in brickwork,
no skilled ledgewise shuffle, gripping
of surrounds, fingertipping the glacial facades,
no bracing against the sudden undercurrent
of wind-tunnel East-River gusts.

In the eerie absence of sirens and klaxons
miles above the tiny gridlocked street-plan
there's only a gentle hum in the rigging,
the whirr of rotary squeegees and brushes,
muted immutabilities of water and soap.

They'll be through this shift by midday,
too deep into the rhythm to register
the blip of the first plane against the blue.

# Guest Information Folder

*You can check out any time you like, but you can never leave...*
*– The Eagles, Hotel California*

*Place shower curtain inside bath.* Don't
confide in night porters. They've sat through too many
David Lynch endings.
                              'Seventies carpets conceal
trails of blood droplets. Avoid washbasin mirrors
with a web of fractures that spin out
from what looks like a single bullet-hole. Order
the Club Sandwich.
                              Delegates' footfalls are vacuumed into
oblivion.
                    Human hairballs get routinely missed.

Tray-breakfasts are lost in transition: half-consumed
debris on plates line Sunday morning corridors
alongside *your choice of daily newspaper.*

Sudden Hitchcockian shadows on half-lit
lone corridors are not a hazard. *In the interests
of your health and safety please note.*
The higher the room the shorter the fall. Cable TVs
are permanently on weather, on mute. Never accept
the room you're offered. Officially you don't exist.
*Have you phoned home today?*

Hotel lifts clank all night and toilet cisterns struggle
to refill by morning.
                              Bedside notepads have spidery thoughts
from the last month's occupants, the phone blinks
with muffled voicemails from other men's wives.

There's always a half-eaten Oreo
pushed back in a wrapper.
                              Not all bellhops
and shoe-shine boys are saving for college. *Remember
you are our number one priority.*

## Into the Dark

Closed doors are always a blessing.
And all the better for staying shut.
Like the bolted door in a secret
garden's wall, the thousand
and one entrances in Arabian tales,
a simple one that opened
on a grove of white crosses
in an Angers convent's grounds,
or the one that finally found me
under a stormy July moon
stumbling through trailing creepers,
spiked by spiny yucca, hands
grazed on monkey-puzzle bark
in next door's exotically inappropriate
Rangoon garden.
                I've tried counting
the freighted, impassive doorways
that have passed themselves off
as untold promise since then, tried asking
if there's any sight on earth so robust, so
assuring, as a door slammed tight.

# While You Wait

Way back, I committed the topography
of a Yale's unforgiving profile to mind,
each serrated tooth, each peak and gap
I could have drawn in my sleep a thousand
times, a whodunit key that would never
be used to unlock a winter boathouse.

No clues as to what lock-type – mortice
or five-lever – it'll spring when I find it
but its imprinted pattern still promises
vital unlockings, long forgotten
bequests, a safe-deposit holding
every silvered trinket I've ever lost...

which is why you find me in the fifth
hardware emporium in as many days,
each shop-coated ironmonger
with his absolute refusal to work
from my sketches: *Where did you
get something like this?*
                          Until now,
in this Aladdin's Cave a block or two
off Main, and not far from Platt
County Correctional, the cool-hand
on the key-grinder admits he enjoys
the more challenging medium
and I unwrap my committed key's reverse
carved in a green carbolic soap-cake.

## Sangre de Cristo

A night, it really is, such a night.
A tequila sunset sinks
behind rows of tombstone cacti.

So we send for blue-black nachos
and pimento salsa to match the fiesta lanterns
flaming the starched fiery tablecloths.

And all night a cherry-red pickup
festooned with ribbons and balloons
swerves up and down the *camino*
blasting into the searing heavy air
election promises we can't quite translate.

Children in Party-red sashes scatter cactus-blooms
for the thorn-crowned, scapegoat Jesus
borne aloft *con pasión* through
the town's foot-worn cobbled alleyways.

Outside the *Mercado* a fountain gushes crimson
through the night of the Feast
of the Most Precious Blood until dawn comes
with its chilled malls and tyre depots.

# Lower Manhattan

And still they come, out of elevators with only
minus-number keypads, through manholes, airshafts,
basement doors that cry 'KEEP OUT, DANGER'.

They arrive, unbidden, in their multitudes, legions,
to blacked-out windows a thousand storeys deep.

Leagues and leagues below subway and sidewalk,
every bleak morning's a silver-sun vigil
as elders with watch-fobs spin dank tales,
shell pistachios on dim-lit storefront benches.

Listen in stairwells and you'll hear a subway's roar,
fire trucks in South Ferry, a rattling coathanger.

Realtors' signboards announce apartments for rent
in upper floors, unclaimed, tenantless,
their marble door-plaques as yet unlettered.

It's been here aeons, the Empire State's inverted
subterranean shadow-land.
                              Since the big expansion.
Everybody knows. And still the glossy horses' plumes
nod
            towards a lifeless arctic midnight sun.

## Acknowledgements

Acknowledgements are due to the editors of the following publications in which some of these poems first appeared: *Manhattan Review*, *New Ohio Review*, *Ocean State Review*, *Ploughshares*, *The Lake*, *The Same*, *The SHOp*.